THE PICTURE LIFE OF TINA TURNER
BY GENE BUSNAR

A GROLIER COMPANY

FRANKLIN WATTS
NEW YORK | LONDON | TORONTO | SYDNEY
1987

Cover photograph courtesy of Bob Leafe/Star File.
Photographs courtesy of Bob Gruen/Star File: pp. 4, 9, 16 (bottom),
26 (bottom), 30 (bottom), 44, 47, 49 (bottom), 52; Ralph Dominguez/
Globe Photos: pp. 6, 43; Donald Sanders/Globe Photos:
pp. 8, 53; David Redfern/Retna Ltd.: pp. 16 (top), 21,
30 (top); Mick Rock/Star File: p. 22; UPI/Bettmann
Newsphotos: p. 26 (top); George Pejoves/Retna Ltd.: p. 32;
Paul Natkin/Star File: p. 35; John Bellissimo/Retna Ltd.:
p. 36; Lisa Seifert/Star File: p. 39; Michael Putland/
Retna Ltd.: p. 40; Vinnie Zuffante/Star File: p. 46 (top);
Andrea Lubach/Retna Ltd.: p. 46 (bottom); Larry Busacca/
Retna Ltd.: p. 49 (top); Scott Weiner/Retna Ltd.: pp. 50, 57;
© 1985 Warner Brothers, Inc., Capital Records: p. 51 (top);
Dee Tosa/Retna Ltd.: pp. 51 (bottom), 58; Chuck Pulin/Star
File: p. 55 (top); Gary Gershoff/Retna Ltd.: p. 55 (bottom).

Library of Congress Cataloging-in-Publication Data

Busnar, Gene.
The picture life of Tina Turner.

Bibliography: p.
Includes index.
Summary: Discusses the life, career, and
accomplishments of the veteran rock singer who
has been performing since the late 1950s and
is enjoying a revival in popularity.
1. Turner, Tina—Juvenile literature. 2. Rock
musicians—United States—Biography—Juvenile
literature. [1. Turner, Tina. 2. Singers.
3. Afro-Americans—Biography. 4. Rock music]
I. Title.
ML3930.T87B9 1987   784.5′4′00924 [B] [92]   86-24717
ISBN 0-531-10297-1

THE PICTURE LIFE
OF TINA TURNER

Tina Turner has been one of rock's best singers and live performers for years. But before Tina became the superstar she is today, she went through a long and difficult struggle.

Tina survived a broken home, a divorce that left her nearly penniless, and a music industry that did not recognize how great her talent was. Finally, after twenty years of turning out powerful records and giving sensational live performances, Tina Turner has made it all the way to the top.

Tina has won many awards for her records and videos. She was voted *Rolling Stone* magazine's best female singer in 1984 and 1985 by both readers and critics. Tina's song "What's Love Got to Do with It" was only one of several big hits from her *Private Dancer* album. It won a Grammy Award as best song of the year—one of the highest honors in the music business.

Tina's latest album is called *Break Every Rule.* It includes hit songs like "Typical Male," "Girls," "Overnight Sensation," and "Back Where You Started."

Aside from her own records and videos, Tina has also recorded duets with other superstars like Bryan Adams, Mick Jagger, David Bowie, and Dire Straits' Mark Knopfler.

Once Tina achieved the kind of success she had been after in her music career, she began to branch out into other fields. She has starred in movies and has written a best-selling book called *I, Tina*. Tina Turner has come a very long way, both as a person and as a performer.

Early Years

Tina's real name is Anna Mae Bullock. She was born on November 26, 1939, in Nutbush, Tennessee, a small town about fifty miles from Memphis. For the first few years of her life, Anna lived with her father, her mother, and her older sister, Eileen. Because she was small and the baby of the family, Anna was nicknamed "Teeny" or "Tina."

Like many other black people in the South, Tina's parents worked on other people's farms picking cotton and fruit. By the time Tina was six, she was working in the fields alongside her father, mother, and sister.

Tina with Lionel Richie at the Grammy Awards presentation.

Above: Tina's newest achievement, her autobiography, I, Tina. Left: the future looks exciting for Tina.

"I was brought up as a country girl," Tina recalls. This is how she remembers her childhood in the song "Nutbush City Limits":

Go to the fields on weekdays . . .
Go to town on Saturday,
Go to church every Sunday.

"My daddy was the caretaker on a plantation," Tina told an interviewer. "People worked for him and he answered to the boss. Every day, [we] went to the fields."

On days when they weren't working, the Bullocks went into the town of Nutbush. Actually, Nutbush wasn't much of a town. It had only one church, one gas station, and one country store where the local farmers bought their supplies.

Life was tough in small southern towns like Nutbush, Tennessee. Still, Tina's family lived better than most of their neighbors. The house Tina grew up in was small, but it was clean and well cared for. Tina and her sister, Eileen, each had her own bedroom. That was a luxury few of the Bullocks' friends could afford.

Because their house was surrounded by a little piece of farmland, the Bullocks were able to raise a few chickens and grow their own vegetables. Tina's family may not have had a great deal, but at least there was steady work and food on the table.

Tina's love for music began when she was quite small. "I was always singing," Tina remembers, "out in the fields picking cotton, around the house."

Like many young black people in the South, Tina also did a good deal of singing at the local Baptist church. That kind of church music is very emotional. It also has a strong, rocking beat.

"I used to really get involved in the church thing," Tina recalls. "The dancing and the carrying on. I didn't understand what it was all about. But the music and the feeling moved me. It's the same way on stage, even today. The music starts and I have to move."

By the time she was eight, Tina was known as a gifted young singer. At school, she sang in the chorus and at talent shows. In the summers, there were town picnics, and Tina was often called upon to entertain.

Everyone in Nutbush came to those summer picnics. They enjoyed eating barbecue, drinking lemonade, and listening to the traveling musicians who were passing through. Tina never missed a chance to sing with those musicians.

For a time, Tina's childhood was quite happy. There were some problems, however. Tina never did care for school all that much. She also didn't like the way she looked.

"I was very thin when I was growing up," Tina told *Ebony* magazine. "I had long legs, high cheekbones (inherited from her mother, who is half Cherokee Indian), and a big mouth. It all just wasn't very stylish back then, especially in Tennessee."

When Tina was eleven, her parents split up. That was the beginning of a very unsettling time for Tina and her sister. First, their mother left Nutbush for St. Louis. A few months later, their father moved to Chicago.

Even though both of their parents had left, Tina and Eileen remained in Tennessee. They lived with different relatives and friends for a time. Finally, the girls moved in with their grandmother, who died when Tina was fourteen. At that point, Tina and Eileen went to live with their mother in St. Louis.

Tina was happy about this move. She had been dreaming about the glamour and excitement of the big city for a long time. At last, she was going to be part of it.

"I always wanted to leave the fields," Tina remembers. "Tennessee was fine. I loved sitting under a tree at the end of the day, but I knew there was more. That's why I joined my mother in St. Louis. To me, that was the big city."

Soon after Tina and her sister arrived, Eileen took a job in a hospital. Then Tina did the same. Some nights after work, Eileen would go to nightclubs in East St. Louis to hear music. Pretty soon, sixteen-year-old Tina started tagging along. Tina and Eileen liked all the nightclubs, but their favorite was the Club Manhattan.

For years, the Club Manhattan had been the most popular nightclub in East St. Louis. Tina had never seen so many good-looking women in fine dresses and sharply dressed men in flashy suits.

The band at the Club Manhattan was called the Kings of Rhythm. Tina thought they were the best and most exciting group of musicians she had ever heard. The leader of the Kings of Rhythm was a keyboard and guitar player named Ike Turner.

The Ike & Tina Turner Revue

By the time Tina and Eileen arrived in St. Louis, Ike was well known as one of the best rhythm and blues musicians around. "Rhythm and blues" is another name for black popular music.

Back in the early fifties, there were three kinds of popular music: pop, country, and rhythm and blues. In those days, records by black musicians like Ike Turner were only played on black radio stations. Since their music was not heard by the much larger white audience, black musicians did not make a lot of money back then.

Important changes began to take place in the record business during the mid-fifties. For the first time, young people had enough money to buy their own records. As it turned out, rhythm and blues was the only kind of popular music that had the beat and feeling young people wanted to hear.

Before long, a handful of rhythm and blues and country musicians began to shape a new sound. It was music created with young people in mind—music with a stronger beat and wilder feel than most people had ever heard before. This music was called rock and roll.

Ike Turner was one of the people who helped invent this new sound. In fact, some music experts believe that a record called "Rocket 88" was the first rock and roll song. The record label lists saxophone player Jackie Brenston as the recording artist on this number-one rhythm and blues hit. But it was Ike Turner who wrote, played piano, and led the band on "Rocket 88."

While Ike was well-known in the world of rhythm and blues, Tina had never even performed in a club. Nevertheless, she had great confidence in her talent. Tina had no doubt that she was good enough to perform with the Kings of Rhythm. That's what gave her the courage to ask Ike to let her sing.

Ike promised to give Tina a chance, but he never did ask her to come onstage. "One night he [Ike] was playing organ, and the drummer put a microphone in front of my sister for her to sing," Tina told an interviewer from *People* magazine. "[Eileen] said no. Then I took the microphone and started singing. Ike was shocked. . . . He couldn't believe that [such a big] voice was coming out of this frail little body."

Tina performed several numbers with the Kings of Rhythm that night. Ike was so impressed that he asked Tina to join the band. At first, Tina just sang with the group on weekends. But before long, she became the star attraction of the Kings of Rhythm.

For a while, Tina worked two jobs. During the day, she continued to work at the hospital. At

Right: Ike and Tina Turner were a winning combination. Below: the Ikettes

night, she would sing with the Kings of Rhythm.

In 1960, Tina started traveling with Ike and the band full time. Later that year, they had their first hit together. Though they were not married, Ike had renamed the band The Ike & Tina Turner Revue.

Ike and Tina's first hit song was called "Fool in Love." Tina wound up singing on that record almost by accident. When the person who was supposed to sing didn't show up for the recording session, Tina was asked to fill in. "Fool in Love" became the first of many rhythm and blues hits for Ike and Tina. Soon Tina was making money and tasting the glamorous life.

"At first, I only made a little spending money," Tina told *People* magazine:

Then Ike started buying me a wardrobe. I had rings all over my fingers and bare-backed shoes. There were Buicks and Cadillacs. It was all very exciting for a young girl like me.

Before long, Ike and Tina started going together. A few months later, Ike proposed marriage. Tina remembers how Ike acted when he went to ask her mother for permission to get married. "He came to her very respectfully,"

Tina told *People.* "Ike said he'd take care of me, and my mother gave her consent."

Ike and Tina got married in 1964. That same year, they moved from St. Louis to Los Angeles. Around that time, too, they had a son named Ronnie. Tina had already given birth to another son named Raymond Craig, whose father played saxophone in Ike's band. Ike also had two other sons. Although Tina was the mother of only one of Ike's children, she helped raise all four boys.

No matter what else was going on in their personal lives, Ike and Tina never stopped working and recording. Although they were doing quite well as a rhythm and blues act, Ike and Tina were still unknown to a large part of the record-buying public.

Then in 1966, Tina made one of the most important records of the sixties. However, she didn't make that record with Ike. She made it with a songwriter and record producer named Phil Spector. A record producer is the person who coordinates the music on a record and decides how it will sound—plain or fancy—smooth or rough.

At the time, Phil Spector was recognized as the best record producer in all of popular music. He was known as the man who invented a style of recording called the "wall of sound." To make simple rock and roll songs more powerful, he used up to eighty instruments on some of his records. Even though the beat was rock and roll, the music on Phil Spector's records often sounded as big as an entire orchestra.

Phil Spector had co-written a song called "River Deep—Mountain High." There was no doubt in his mind that Tina Turner was the singer to record it. Although the record label reads "Ike & Tina Turner," Ike actually had nothing to do with "River Deep—Mountain High." Tina does recall, however, that Mick Jagger dropped in to the recording session.

Tina's performance on that record was more than a match for Phil Spector's powerful "wall of sound." In fact, Tina's singing on "River Deep—Mountain High" is often cited as one of the great all-time performances by a female singer. Her special mixture of emotional power and toughness has rarely been equaled.

As great as it was, "River Deep— Mountain High" never did become a big hit in America. "Black stations thought it was too pop," Tina has often explained, "and white stations thought it was too black."

Phil Spector was so disappointed and angry at the lack of success by the record in this country that he quit the record business for a few years. Spector was often quoted as saying that the American public simply did not deserve the great music he was offering.

In spite of the disappointing sales of "River Deep—Mountain High" in America, there was good news from overseas. The record had reached number three on the English hit parade. Before long, "River Deep—Mountain High" also became a big hit in several other countries.

In time, the record would sell over a million copies worldwide. Phil Spector still wasn't happy. But as far as Ike and Tina were concerned, the record had put them on the map. This was just the break they had been waiting for.

Ike and Tina soon became big international stars. No matter how slowly things were going in America, The Ike & Tina Turner Revue was always in demand in England, other European countries, and Australia.

Ike and Tina toured with The Rolling Stones in 1966 and again in 1968 and 1969. Those tours helped the Turners polish their act and exposed them to an entire new generation of rock listeners.

Tina's performance of the song "I've Been Loving You Too Long" in the 1970 Rolling

Ike and Tina appear on a British television show.

Tina has always poured out her heart and soul when performing.

Stones movie *Gimme Shelter* attracted large numbers of new fans. Even Mick Jagger had to admit that he had rarely seen a performer move an audience the way Tina could. In fact, Mick has confessed that he learned how to dance onstage by watching Tina and her backup singers, The Ikettes.

"I don't think [Jagger] copied," Tina told an interviewer from a magazine called *The Face*:

> *He was [fascinated] by our dancing because at the start of his career he didn't move—he just beat his tambourine. But he probably always wanted to dance. When we were touring, he'd ask: "How do your girls dance?" Now he's doing it and he's doing it his way.*

Once rock audiences were given a taste of what Ike and Tina could do, they wanted more. To fill that demand, Ike and Tina kept up a very active performing and recording schedule over the next few years. They had a string of hit records in the late sixties and early seventies. Many of those hits were remakes of rock and roll songs that originally had been recorded by other bands.

The Turners' versions of songs like the Beatles' "Come Together," John Fogerty's

"Proud Mary," and The Rolling Stones' "Honky Tonk Woman" sold very well.

Sometimes the music on Ike and Tina's records wasn't all that different from the original versions. Still, Tina always gave every song her own special vocal treatment. She gave a pretty good description of her singing style at the beginning of "Proud Mary." As Ike sang the first verse of the song in a low bass voice, Tina growled:

> *You know, sometimes people say they'd like to hear us do something nice and easy. . . . But there's just one thing: We never, ever do anything nice and easy. . . . So we're going to take this song and do it nice—and rough!*

The Turners were finally reaching the audience that Ike had been after since the early fifties. But there were personal problems between the couple that would soon cause the breakup of both their act and their marriage.

Ike Turner was a talented musician, but there was no doubt that Tina was the star of The Ike & Tina Turner Revue. Ike knew that it was good business to feature Tina on their records and live performances. But Ike could never truly accept that he was less important than the young girl he had discovered.

24

Musicians who worked with the band describe Ike as the kind of person who always had to be in charge. Ike made all the decisions—onstage and off. When Tina disagreed with him or questioned his authority, Ike would become very angry. He would often lose his temper and hit her.

From the outside, people saw Tina living the life of a star. She had diamonds, furs, and fancy cars. But, in fact, Tina usually felt more like Ike's servant than his business and musical partner.

"Ike was so mixed up with anger and confusion," Tina has said. "Sometimes after he beat me up, I'd end up feeling sorry for him. Maybe I was brainwashed."

The Breakup

As the years passed, Tina became more and more unhappy about her life with Ike. She often wondered what good her stardom was if she had no dignity and no control of her life. Tina knew that there was only one solution to her problem: At some point, she would have to find the strength to walk out on her marriage.

In 1975, the Turners' string of hit records came to an end. Tina realized that this was as good a time as any to split with Ike. "I was

Right: Tina hugging composer-singer Neil Sedaka at a 1978 party
Below: Tina and her sons

unhappy with the type of material I was doing,"
she recalled. "My sons had grown up, and it
was time to leave."

As Tina expected, Ike became angry when
she told him that she was walking out after
sixteen years. But Tina was not afraid of Ike's
threats. Instead, she became more determined
than ever to go ahead with her plans.

When Tina left Ike, she only had thirty-six
cents and a gasoline credit card in her pocket.
But there was no question in Tina's mind that
she was doing the right thing. "I felt proud,"
Tina remembers. "I felt strong. I felt like Martin
Luther King."

A few months later, Tina filed for a divorce.
She asked for no money, no property, and no
payback for the years she had put into building
The Ike & Tina Turner Revue. Ike got the house
and all their other property, but that was fine
with Tina. She was ready and willing to give up
anything in order to free herself from a bad
situation.

Tina had her freedom and peace of mind at
last. Unfortunately, there were other problems.
After her divorce, Tina went through a tough
period. She was alone and almost completely
broke. To make matters worse, she was also

without any work as a singer for the first time in years.

In a 1984 interview in the New York *Daily News*, Tina remembered how confused she felt:

> *I stopped [working]. I rented a house and second-hand furniture. . . . At night, I'd look at the stars in the sky instead of at concert lights. It was almost a year until I could even think about going back to work.*

Tina admits that she had so much on her mind after her breakup with Ike that she could not keep her mind on her career. She had to find a place to live, support her teenage sons, and build a new life for herself. It wasn't easy, but Tina never lost faith that things would take a turn for the better.

For a while, Tina lived with some women friends who introduced her to Buddhist chanting. The religious teachings of Buddhism helped Tina a great deal. She continues to believe in them today.

After a year of rest, Tina felt much stronger in mind and body. She still had very little money and needed to get back to work. Naturally, she wanted to return to singing. But there were few offers to perform or record. Tina was surprised to find that many doors were completely closed to her.

The Ike & Tina Turner Revue had been in the middle of a tour when Tina left Ike. Concerts had to be canceled, and many thousands of dollars were lost. Ike let everyone know that it was Tina who had walked out, and she was held responsible. Until Tina could pay back that lost money, many people in the music business were simply not willing to hire her.

In order to pay off her debts, Tina was forced to accept whatever bookings she could find. Most of these jobs were far below the level she had reached working with Ike.

After performing in large concert halls all over the world, Tina was not happy about having to work at business conventions and in Las Vegas lounges. But neither was she ashamed. Tina considered herself a professional. And when times are tough, a professional has to be prepared to work anywhere.

It would take Tina eight years to pay off all her debts, but that didn't bother her. She had always been a hard worker, and she wasn't about to stop now. Tina knew that in time, she would be able to put her money problems behind her. But she also knew that it would take much more to satisfy her.

Tina is a versatile, emotional entertainer.

During a tour of France in 1985
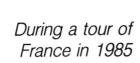

Once she was back on her feet, Tina wanted to become a star on her own. She never doubted that she would succeed. But she also knew that the road was not going to be easy.

Tina Turner's Comeback

During her years with Ike, Tina had more than proven her talent as a singer and performer. But she hadn't done some of the other things that make performers successful.

Before even a great singer like Tina Turner can make a record or walk out onto a stage, there is a lot of work that has to be done by other people. Somebody has to pick the musicians, write the songs, and make sure that everybody gets paid. In the past, all of those details had been handled by Ike. Now Tina had to take care of them herself.

Tina quickly discovered that she had learned a great deal about running a band from watching Ike, and that gave her confidence. No matter how bad things became, she always managed to keep working.

Tina never stopped believing in herself as a performer. She knew she could reach audiences, whether they were in a concert hall

or a second-rate nightclub. But Tina also understood that to really be successful, she would need to record a hit album on her own.

During Ike and Tina Turner's years as a team, neither of them had ever written a song that became a big hit outside of the rhythm and blues market. Unlike some recording artists, Tina had never been that interested in writing songs and producing records. She had written a few good songs during her time with Ike, "Nutbush City Limits," for one. For the most part, though, Tina concentrated on what she did best—singing and performing.

Tina realized that in order to make it to the top, she would need the help of a good record producer, good songwriters, and a good manager. A manager's job is to help a performer plan her career so that she will perform in good places and get paid fairly.

During the eight years between her breakup with Ike in 1976 and her comeback in 1984, Tina worked with several managers and record producers. Although she did make some records during those years, Tina wasn't getting the kind of results she was looking for.

In concert

During the early eighties, many people wondered why a great artist like Tina Turner wasn't really making it. After all, she sang and performed as well as ever. Why, then, couldn't Tina find a top producer or a record company who knew how to bring out her talents?

"The record companies say I'm doing all old material," Tina complained to a reporter from *The New York Sunday News Magazine* in 1981. "But you have to give audiences what they want. . . .

"I've had a few nibbles [from record companies]. But I'm going to be real selective this time around. I don't want another album on the shelf. I want a record company [that is really] behind me."

Fortunately, Tina had some important friends behind her. Rock superstars like Mick Jagger, Keith Richards, and Rod Stewart had long recognized Tina's greatness. One of the things they did to help bring her to the public's attention was to make Tina the opening act on their arena-size concert tours.

Tina greatly appreciated all this help from her friends. But she sincerely believed that with the

Tina with Mick Jagger

right songs, record producer, and management, she could be the main headliner, not just a great opening act.

In a way, Tina agreed with what the record companies had been saying about her. She probably could have gone on making a living performing her old hits. But this would not bring Tina the kind of recognition she was after. For that to happen, she needed a new musical direction.

"I never wanted to sing and scream and do all of that wailing," Tina told a reporter from *Newsweek*. "But that was how I was produced in the early days by my ex-husband. . . .

> *I realized I liked the way people like Eric Clapton and The Rolling Stones had mixed white and black music, taking feeling from black people and adding it to their own. Blues to me is depressing. [Rock and roll] has a liberating feeling about it and I needed a change.*

Tina knew that the key to shaping a new musical direction was to hook up with a

Tina displays a variety of emotions when she sings.

manager or producer who could help her find hit songs. After several managers did not work out, Tina signed with an Australian manager named Roger Davies. He advised her to stop working nightclubs. Instead, he wanted her to put all her energies into going after a record deal.

Roger Davies introduced Tina to Martyn Ware, Greg Walsh, and Glen Gregory—members of an English band called Heaven 17. In 1982, Tina sang lead on their version of a 1968 Temptations song called "Ball of Confusion." The song was not a big hit in America, but critics and listeners raved about Tina's performance.

In 1983, Tina got together with Heaven 17 again. They recorded "Let's Stay Together," a song that had been a big hit for singer Al Green in 1972.

A few months later, Tina played at a New York City rock club called The Ritz. David Bowie, Keith Richards, and a number of influential record business people were in the audience. Everyone was knocked out by Tina's performance.

Finally, Tina landed the record deal she was after. Capitol records offered Tina a budget of $150,000 to make an album. There was only one problem: Capitol wanted the record finished in two

Backstage at the Ritz in 1983

weeks while the excitement of Tina's performance at The Ritz was still fresh in people's minds.

Most of the time, recording artists are given months to finish their albums. Practically no one can make an entire album in just two weeks. But Tina had no intention of letting this opportunity slip away. One way or another, she was going to record a hit album.

Tina and Roger Davies left immediately for the friendly surroundings of London to begin recording. Throughout her career, Tina had been helped by English musicians, and this time was no exception. Tina and Davies called some friends to ask for songs and production help. The response was fantastic.

Mark Knopfler of Dire Straits gave Tina "Private Dancer," which was to become the album's title song. Heaven 17's Martyn Ware and Greg Walsh produced a dramatic version of David Bowie's "1984." Terry Britten—a friend of Davies' from Australia—wrote and produced several songs on the album, including the award-winning hit "What's Love Got to Do with It."

With Elton John

In just a few short weeks, Tina had recorded one of the most important rock albums of the eighties. Soon she would claim her rightful place as one of the brightest stars in show business.

On Top at Last

By the spring of 1984, Tina was riding high off the success of the *Private Dancer* album. But she was still working to pay off the money she owed. By the end of that summer, every dime was finally paid back. "I have my freedom now," she said at the time. "Everything I have earned, I've earned with my own blood."

It took many years for the public to appreciate Tina's special talents, but now she is recognized as a full-fledged superstar. In recent years, Tina has won Grammy Awards for being the Best Female Pop Vocalist and the Best Female Rock Vocalist. She has also become one of the most popular and successful live performers in rock.

One important reason for Tina's great success is the popularity of her videos. Video

Tina has won several music awards.

*Tina's success in video
has been fantastic.*

hits like "What's Love Got to Do with It," "You'd Better Be Good to Me," and "Private Dancer" gave many new fans the opportunity to see and hear Tina.

"Video is great for me," Tina told *Billboard* magazine after she was selected the top video artist of 1984. "I am a visual performer first, so video is natural for me. I feel right at home with it."

Once Tina started making it big as a radio and video star, she began going after another one of her dreams—acting.

"When I used to work in the fields, I'd daydream about being a movie star," she remembers. "I didn't think about the singing too much because I was already singing then. . . . I wanted to go past that. I wanted to be an actor."

During the seventies, Tina appeared in several movies. Most of these were musicals like *Gimme Shelter*, *Soul to Soul*, and *The Big TNT Show*. Tina was glad to have the chance to work in these films. But she hoped that one day she would be given a real acting role.

Tina finally got the chance to act in the 1975 film *Tommy*. She enjoyed working with people like The Who, Eric Clapton, and actor Jack Nicholson. Tina was praised for her performance

Opposite: Joan Baez, the folksinger, with Tina at a party for the MTV Awards in New York City. Right: Tina accepts Best Female Video award for "What's Love Got to Do with It?" Below: Tina at her Madison Square Garden concert in August 1985.

as "the acid queen" in *Tommy*, but this wasn't exactly the kind of acting she had in mind. *Tommy* was a rock-opera, and Tina wanted a chance to act in something in which she did not have to sing.

"I think I'd be terrific in one of those outer space movies," Tina told an interviewer from *Rolling Stone*. In other interviews, she talked about how badly she wanted a part like the one Grace Jones played in *Conan The Destroyer*.

Even before he read those interviews, Australian film director George Miller had been thinking that Tina would be perfect for the female lead in his film *Mad Max Beyond Thunderdome*. Tina gladly accepted Miller's offer to co-star in that film with Mel Gibson.

Though Tina does not actually sing in the film, she did make a record and video called "We Don't Need Another Hero." The video features Tina dressed as "Aunty Entity," the character she plays in *Mad Max Beyond Thunderdome*.

Today Tina is in great demand as an actress. In fact, she has turned down any number of important parts, including a starring role in the film *The Color Purple*.

After all her years of struggling, Tina now has the freedom to take on only those musical and film projects that really interest her. Recently,

Left: Backstage with
Dave Winfield of the
New York Yankees.
Below: Elton John and
Tina at a Tommy party
in New York.

Performing with Lionel Richie

Top: Tina was a tremendous success in the movie Mad Max Beyond Thunderdome. *Right: Tina puts tremendous energy into her performances.*

Above: a rare moment to relax
Left: Among the famous people whose company Tina enjoys is the French fashion designer Azzedine Alaia, who designs Tina's clothes.

she has turned her attention to helping others who are less fortunate than she. She has given time and energy to causes like world hunger and Amnesty International.

In 1985, Tina joined other concerned performers to form a group called USA for Africa. Together with rock superstars like Stevie Wonder, Huey Lewis, Cyndi Lauper, Ray Charles, Bob Dylan, and Bruce Springsteen, Tina devoted her time and talent to help feed starving people in Africa. The record and video *We Are the World* was one of USA for Africa's most important money-raising projects. The song, written by Lionel Richie and Michael Jackson, won Grammy Awards as the Record of the Year and Song of the Year for 1985. One of the highlights of the *We Are the World* album is Tina singing a song called "Total Control."

In the summer of 1985, Tina took part in Live Aid—a concert devoted to raising money to

Top, right: Tina and Mick Jagger heat up the fans at the Live Aid concert in 1985. Right: Tina in a calm moment on an MTV set

fight world hunger. The performers at that concert included Sting, Madonna, Robert Plant, and Phil Collins.

One of the most exciting moments of the Live Aid concert came when Tina and Mick Jagger sang the Rolling Stones classic "It's Only Rock 'n' Roll." The temperature was almost ninety degrees at the Live Aid concert, but Tina and Mick's performance was even hotter than the steamy weather.

People have always been amazed at the way Tina dances and moves onstage. In terms of pure energy, Tina's dancing may be even more highly charged than her singing. As one concert reviewer remarked, "You can work up a sweat just watching her."

It's not easy for a woman in her forties to be a rock star. But age means nothing to Tina. She has more energy and drive than most people half her age.

Tina credits her good health and terrific figure to keeping active and staying away from drugs, alcohol (except for white wine occasionally), and cigarettes. At 5 feet 4 inches and a slim 125 pounds, Tina is careful about her diet. However, she does not jog or have a regular exercise program. As Tina told *Life* magazine, "The dancing I do onstage, and running for planes with my bags is all the exercise I need."

These days, Tina's life is busier than ever before. When she's not performing on the road, she's in the studio recording a new song or shooting a new video. Then there is her acting career and her book.

What can we expect from Tina Turner in the future? There will surely be more great records, more videos, more films, and more dynamite concerts. There will probably also be a few surprises.

"People keep asking me when I'm going to slow down," says Tina. "I tell them that I'm just getting started."

SELECTED DISCOGRAPHY
ALBUMS: TINA TURNER

Break Every Rule .... Capitol
Mad Max Beyond Thunderdome .... Capitol
Private Dancer .... Capitol
Rough ....UA
Tommy .... Polydor
We Are the World
(USA for Africa) .... Columbia

SINGLES: TINA TURNER

''Better Be Good to Me/When I Was
  Young'' .... Capitol
''I Wrote a Letter'' .... Capitol
''It's Only Love'' with Bryan Adams ....A&M
''Let's Pretend We're Married'' .... Capitol
''Let's Stay Together'' .... Capitol
''One of the Living'' .... Capitol
''Private Dancer'' .... Capitol
''Nutbush City Limits'' .... Capitol
''Rock 'n' Roll Widow'' .... Capitol
''Show Some Respect'' .... Capitol
''Typical Male'' .... Capitol
''We Are the World''
(USA for Africa) .... Columbia

"We Don't Need Another
Hero" *(Thunderdome)* .... Capitol
"What's Love Got to Do with It" .... Capitol
"When I Was Young" .... Capitol

VIDEOS

"It's Only Love" with Bryan Adams 1986
"We Don't Need Another Hero" 1985
"Private Dancer" 1984
"We Are the World" 1985
"What's Love Got to Do
with It" 1984
"You'd Better Be Good to Me" 1984
"Ball of Confusion" 1983
"Let's Stay Together" 1983
"Nice 'n' Rough" 1981

FILMS

Mad Max Beyond Thunderdome 1985
Tommy 1975
*Rock City/Sound of
the City* 1973
Soul to Soul 1971
Gimme Shelter 1971

Taking Off (comedy)...................................... 1971
Superstars in Film Concert........................... 1971
It's Your Thing 1970
The Big TNT Show 1966

ALBUMS: IKE & TINA TURNER

Acid Queen..UA
Black Man Soul...Pompeii
Come Together ....UA
Don't Play Me Cheap ....SUE
Festival of Live Performances ....Kent
Greatest Hits..UA
Live at Carnegie Hall ....UA
'Nuff Said ....UA
Nutbush City Limits ....UA
Proud Mary ....Liberty
River Deep—Mountain High........................A&M
Sixteen Great Performances ....ABC
Shame Shame Shame............................Fantasy
The Best of Ike
and Tina Turner ....Blue Thumb
What You Hear Is What You Get....................UA
Workin' Together.......................................Liberty
World of Ike and Tina Turner ....UA

SINGLES: IKE & TINA TURNER

"Bold Soul Sister" .... Blue Thumb
"Come Together" .... Minit
"River Deep—Mountain High" .... A&M
"Ooh Poo Pah Doo" .... UA
"Proud Mary" .... Liberty
"The Hunter" .... Blue Thumb

FOR FURTHER READING

Busnar, Gene. *The Rhythm and Blues Story*.
    New York: Julian Messner, 1985.

Ivory, Steven. *Tina*. New York: Perigee Books,
    1985.

Mills, Bart. *Tina*. New York: Warner Books, 1985.

Turner, Tina, with Loder, Kurt. *I, Tina*. New York:
    William Morrow, 1986.

INDEX